LIVING THE JUCHE LIE
North Korea's Kim Dynasty

By James G. Zumwalt

I0115596

FⲞRTIS

A NON-FICTION IMPRINT FROM ADDUCENT
Adducent, Inc.
www.Adducent.co

Titles Distributed In
North America
United Kingdom
Western Europe
South America
Australia

Living the Juche Lie
North Korea's Kim Dynasty

By James G. Zumwalt

ISBN 978-1-937592-18-9

Published by Adducent, Inc. under its Fortis non-fiction imprint

Jacksonville, Florida

www.Adducent.co (*that's right, it's not a .com*)

Published in the United States of America

The Evolution of Power to Yet Another Generation of Kims—And the Conditions Giving Rise To It

The December 28, 2011 photographs of tens of thousands of North Koreans lining the streets of Pyongyang, uncontrollably mourning the passing of their leader, Kim Jong Il, as his hearse drove by, underscore the Kim family's success in its uninterrupted 63-year rule of the country. It stems from their mastery in molding the psyche of the masses they have led. The process began with the rise to power of Kim Jong Il's father and the nation's founder, Kim Il Sung, who, before his death in 1994 at age 82, had taught his son well. The family's future success in continuing its rule now turns on Kim Jong Il's youngest, most favored son (the second son of Kim Jong Il's third wife, opera star Ko Young Hee) "Crown Prince" Kim Jong Un, mastering the same process. Should he fail to, which is highly unlikely, turbulent times could be in store for the peninsula.

What follows seeks to provide the reader with insights into the mindset of Pyongyang's leadership and the North Korean people whom, contrary to man's instinctive nature to cast off the yoke of oppression, either choose not to or, those few moved to do so, simply lack the ability to organize against it. Such insights will underscore what impact the death of Kim Jong Il and the transition to power of his Kim Jong Il's son means for the Koreas and the US. In understanding this mindset, one should come to recognize the real tragedy on the Korean peninsula is, despite Pyongyang's history of aggression primarily against South Korea, for as long as the Kim Dynasty survives, it is the people of North Korea who remain its real victims.

A Leadership Process that Baffles the Outside World

The effectiveness of the leadership process has worked for the Kims ever since the Soviet Union helped usher in Kim Il Sung as North Korea's first head-of-state in 1948. While all other communist states (save Cuba) function within a system by which Party members, unrelated to the leader, compete for the country's leadership role, North Korean military and Party leaders have embraced a "royalty" system by which succeeding generations of Kims are enthroned and worshipped.

Such a system of government has blinded the North Korean people to what is all too visible to outside observers. The outside world peers in through a window exposing the very soul of Pyongyang's leadership as evidenced by how Pyongyang cares for its own people. What it sees is most worrisome: North Korean leadership not only fails to provide to its people the basic necessities for daily survival; but when the people have endeavored to provide for themselves giving rise to a successful black market, the government attempts to wrestle control away. Such control, based on Pyongyang's economic track record, would be a death knell for their productivity. Clearly, a mismanaged economy, combined with a set of laws where the most innocent acts of citizens—such as allowing dust to accumulate on framed photographs of Kim Il Sung and Kim Jong Il displayed in every government building and many private homes—is criminal is not conducive to the people's wellbeing or to stimulating their creativity to fend for themselves under an irresponsible leadership.

The process is inexplicable because there is little positive return the people have to show for being subjected to one family rule for so long.

The *Juche* Tower

An Empty Economic Policy Belies *Juche's* Sinister Purpose

Millions of North Koreans have died in famines unnecessarily induced by a leadership promoting a shell of an economic concept known as the "*Juche Idea.*" *Juche* means independence in everything. It means independence in politics, self-sufficiency in economy and self-reliance in national defense. But, from the economic perspective, juche is a policy devoid of substance. The Party line's drumbeat of *juche* is pounded into people's heads, suggesting all they need to survive exists within their own borders. However, despite its lack of economic success for decades, Pyongyang's leadership is still committed to making it a reality. One can only wonder how long such insanity will continue.

But *juche's* declared intention belies its real purpose, which is far more sinister. It really represents "leadership survival by omission." Recognizing it is incapable of caring for its people, the leadership ignores any responsibility to do so. The focus, therefore, becomes one of solely improving life for those necessary to help maintain the Kim dynasty's power base. Its survivability becomes tied to living the lie that "juche is the answer," while denying the people the opportunity to know otherwise. Accordingly, it must actively take steps to prevent its people from gaining even an inkling of how much better life is outside its borders. It is the knowledge, within its borders, of the prosperity outside of them that would cause their people to demand a leadership change to get what they have been denied. Juche is a lie that, left to be believed by the North Korean people, provides the means by which they will remain enslaved.

Why Pyongyang Fears Its Closest Ally

There is irony in the fact North Korea's closest ally provides the North Korean leadership with its greatest fear. While China has come to Pyongyang's assistance when Pyongyang repeatedly pressed the limit of South Korean tolerance with acts of aggression, it is something over which neither Pyongyang nor Beijing has control that worries North Korea's leadership the most. It fears their people's access to outside information about China's success--learned by those traversing its borders—will be shared with fellow North Koreans. As more and more North Koreans hear about the prosperity being enjoyed just across the border, it has driven many to risk their lives to cross over into China. But it is the knowledge of China's prosperity being spread to its own citizens that Pyongyang fears most. That is why North Korean defectors—later returned by the Chinese government—are immediately imprisoned to isolate them from the general population.

Juche's Wackiness Reflected by its Architect's Defection

Based on its madcap economic principles, *juche* has generated a disastrous economy and repeated crop failures—the latter to which Mother Nature has contributed as well—leaving North Korea unable to feed itself. Interestingly, the senior North Korean official who is credited with creating *juche*—the late Hwang Jong Yop—defected to South Korea in 1997 after Kim Jong Il came to power. Hwang fully understood the fallacy, and the focus, of his own concept and that Pyongyang committed to continuing its implementation.

Part of Hwang's motivation to defect was perhaps due to his having earlier fallen out of favor with Kim Il Sung. To Kim Il Sung's dismay, Hwang had become too enamored of China's capitalist reforms. But, unwilling to consider anything that would undermine *juche*, Kim Il Sung refused to listen to Hwang, minimizing his role in the country's economy. Knowing his father's dissatisfaction with Hwang, Kim Jong Il had further reduced Hwang's influence.

But Hwang's defection—the highest ranking North Korean official ever to do so—remained a source of embarrassment for Pyongyang. So much so that thirteen years later, the defection still gnawed at Kim Jong Il. In 2010, he dispatched two assassins who, after six months of training, embarked upon an unsuccessful attempt to kill Hwang. (State-ordered assassinations by Pyongyang in the South of defectors from the North had some success as evidenced by the 1997 murder of the nephew of Kim Jong Il's mistress.) Later informed of the attempt on his life, Hwang responded, "Death is just death. There is no difference from dying of old age or being killed by Kim Jong Il." It is an attitude seemingly shared by the fellow citizens he left behind who, having failed yet to rise up against the Kim dynasty, accept their fate that, "Death is just death"—even when caused by starvation. (Fatefully, four months after the two assassins were sentenced by a South Korean court to ten years in prison, Hwang died in October 2010, at the age of 87; old age accomplished what Kim Jong Il could not.)

Entrepreneurial Flicker Among the Economic Ruins of *Juche*

With 70% of its trade with China and the balance with Russia, North Korea's economy would be in total collapse were it not for a flicker of entrepreneurial spirit that has sprung up in the country. *Juche's* complete failure as an economic policy is further evidenced by a 200% rise in the cost of rice occurring between November 2009 and the end of 2011. As a result, it has generated an informal, initially underground but now more open, black market. Paradoxically, where economic success has flourished, Pyongyang has tried to contain it since that prosperity exists independent of the leadership's control. But, partly because underpaid

North Korean security forces accept bribes to look the other way, it continues somewhat unabated. It is estimated without this black market a shocking 70% of the people would lack anything to eat. Disrupting that market—even for a short period of time—would have a devastating impact on the North Korean people. Yet, Pyongyang's leadership is still focused on gaining control over it.

An NPR interview with some North Korean experts emphasized Pyongyang's leadership has little interest in economic reform. And, even if it did, it lacks the institutional capacity to make them work. Thus, we should not be hopeful Chinese-style reforms will evolve there under a Kim Jong Un regime as, historically, in launching economic reforms; the country has been unable to handle them well.

Billions for Nukes but not One Cent to Feed the People

Pyongyang has invested into its nuclear weapons program, billions of dollars that should have gone into improving life for its citizens. The only thing the leadership has proven capable of feeding its people is *juche*, while rattling its nuclear sword or undertaking acts of violence to blackmail the international community—blinded by hopes of buying peace in our time—into meeting its food demands. More often than not, such supplies are then confiscated by Pyongyang to feed its army.

In discussing Pyongyang's nukes, it is important to understand the threat North Korea poses. Unlike Iran, which when it obtains nuclear arms is likely to use them, Pyongyang's threat is one of selling nuclear arms technology. It has done so to Iran as well as to Syria. Concerned about Syria's nuclear arms program, Israel launched a strike in 2007 against a not-yet completed facility, destroying it, that resulted in the world not having to deal with a nuclear-armed Syria today.

Evolution of North Korea's "Hobbit" Army

Not even the military has proven immune from suffering under *juche*. For decades, physical standards for recruits have repeatedly been lowered so as to create qualified candidates to serve. Today's height standards are an unbelievable 53.9 inches—just shy of 4' 6 "—as generations of North Koreans have suffered through famines. As a consequence, the North Korean military is truly evolving into an army of "hobbits." Yet, only 120 miles to the south from Pyongyang, an abundance of food has caused height and weight standards for South Korea's military steadily to increase.

Food has been so scarce, many people are forced to eat grass, the bark off of trees or pick through animal excrement for edible kernels of corn as sustenance. As a third of the country's population remains chronically hungry, severe malnutrition has caused cognitive impairment for millions. It is estimated such impairment is responsible for 17%-29% of all conscripts being rejected. The approach taken by Pyongyang to attack the food problem has been a passive one—i.e., simply to allow enough people to die until it no longer presents a problem for the government.

The measure of a society's prosperity is reflected by the generational increase in the average citizen's height and weight. Under the Kim family's leadership, the trend has been a downward spiral—and it is doubtful the direction will change for the next generation.

Yet, as their own people starve, Kim dynasty members have feasted on lobster and a favorite of the late Kim Jong Il—roasted donkey meat. Out of touch with his own people, Kim Jong Il was ordering $700,000 worth of cognac annually as North Korean children were being marred for life by malnutrition. While many more donkeys will now survive due to the death of Kim Jong Il, whether many more North Koreans will depends on the direction Kim Jong Un decides to take his country.

Kim Jong Un—who appears not to have missed many meals himself—will now demand obedience and loyalty from famine survivors who suffered under the rule of his father and grandfather. And, he will receive it. In any other nation where millions died of starvation—estimated as much as nine percent of North Korea's population—there would be riots in the streets. This is unlikely in North Korea—at least for the foreseeable future. Key to any successful effort to turn out the Kim regime would require the cooperation of the army—a very unlikely scenario for the country.

Smaller North Koreans Must Be Easier to Abuse

There is one thing growing inside North Korea's borders under the Kim dynasty and that is the size of its political labor camps to which hundreds of thousands of citizens have been sent. Some inmates do not even know the reason for their incarceration; for others, their only sin has been the defection of a blood relative—such as the fate suffered by Hwang Jong Yop's family. It is a society in which the sins of the father are truly visited upon the son—and beyond. As Kim Il Sung ordered long ago, "Enemies of class, whoever they are, their seed must be eliminated through three generations." A satellite photograph reveals one such camp to be larger than the city of Los Angeles. It is believed recent camp population increases were triggered by Kim Jong Il's effort to sanitize the population of those who might oppose his son's succession.

Pyongyang's Successful Experiment in Mind Control Makes Revolution Unlikely

For 63 years, North Korea—known as the "Hermit Kingdom" for its total isolation from the rest of the world—has proven to be a laboratory experiment in mind control. Three factors critical to the Kims' successful experiment include filtering information flow to the people and building up the Kim family member's image as a deity. Where the first two together fail to have the desired effect, the leadership has turned to the third factor—fear.

The author was a frequent visitor to North Korea from 1994 to 2004, witnessing the first two factors firsthand. Government controlled radio and television stations would spin the information they broadcast to the people, crediting the Kims for all successes while blaming domestic or foreign enemies for all failures. Domestically available radios only received government stations. Efforts to jury rig them for international reception constituted a criminal offense, punishable by death.

Nowhere is the control of information more obvious than by the contents of a massive building in Pyongyang known as the "People's Study Hall." Supposedly North Korea's equivalent of the US Library of Congress, it is a facility where scholars go to learn. However, books and magazines are heavily censored so that opinions formed by readers are only those the leadership wants them to reach. Such limited access by the people to information obviously provides them with little basis for conducting any kind of comparative analysis as to what North Koreans may have or not have vis-à-vis the rest of the world community.

The ability of citizens to communicate among themselves over the years has been severely limited as well. Few private citizens own phones or cars. To further limit communications, for many years even owning a bicycle was illegal. A travel prohibition beyond a six mile radius of one's village sought to limit village residents from communicating with one another. Despite limited transportation, the government feared bicycles only encouraged contact—empowering people to air their dissatisfaction with the government and coordinate anti-government activities.

Although the bicycle prohibition has since been lifted due to a dreadful public transportation system, the lack of communication infrastructure would inhibit any ability to organize anti-government efforts even when North Koreans are motivated to do so.

The Kim dynasty's laboratory experiment in mind control succeeds by keeping their people in total isolation, controlling the flow of information, deifying the leadership and imposing fear where the these other factors fail to achieve the desired result.

It is debatable what the main contributing factor to Pyongyang's success is in fostering the silence and inaction of its people in challenging the suffering they endure. Is it the product of a population's mind so denied information access and otherwise isolated from the world community that people really believe, as they have been programmed to believe, as bad as things are in their country, they are far worse outside of it? Is it simply fear? Or is it a combination of both?

The North Koreans' situation brings to mind an earlier generation's plight in having to choose between inaction—fostered by fear—or acting in spite of it.

It was World War II. Thousands of British Royal Air Force POWs were housed at the Germans' notorious Stalag Luft III camp—immortalized by the 1963 movie "The Great Escape"—where escape was deemed impossible. Up to the challenge, prisoners dug a hundred foot escape tunnel. On the evening of March 24, 1944, one of the biggest prisoner escapes of the war was attempted.

For some, their freedom was short-lived; for most, it was fatal. Only three escapees reached safety. Seventy-three others were re-captured—of which only 23 were returned to the camp. The remaining fifty were lined up alongside a road and shot in the back of the head, executed as an example to others contemplating an escape. The Germans' message was clear—an escape attempt was a death sentence.

Fear obviously is an effective weapon in molding group conduct. But for these prisoners, it proved otherwise. With fear of death looming overhead, they began construction on another tunnel—not as an escape tunnel, but a fighting tunnel. It sought to take the fight to a brutal enemy by gaining access to the German's armory inside the camp compound to access their weapons and fight their way out.

The POWs weighed their fear of death against their loss of freedom—with the scales tilting in favor of the latter. Although there was risk in pursuing it, life without freedom for them was worse than the risk of death fighting for it.

While the Stalag Luft III story is one of courageous men able to overcome their fear of death to fight for their freedom, it involves a critical element missing from the North Korea situation, precisely because Pyongyang's leadership has effectively denied it to them.

The POWs at Stalag Luft III had a taste of something no North Korean, other than defectors, have yet to taste. Born and bred in a free society, the POWs were fully aware of its benefits. They had enjoyed those freedoms to the extent they were willing to fight to the death those denying such benefits unto them.

The average North Korean has no idea what treasures a free society provides. He is unable to comprehend the joys of freedom of choice to do what one wishes free of governmental interference. Having never experienced freedom, he lacks man's natural instinct to lay down his life to fight for it.

An empty stomach can do much to cause one not so inclined to fight for a better life and overcome the fear of death to do so. Whether the North Korean people are capable of reaching that point remains to be seen. But, even so, their leadership denies them the basic tools of communication to the extent necessary to effectively organize anti-government protests. Accordingly, such an effort might well prove fatal before a popular revolution can be mounted. Unfortunately for the people, the Kim dynasty has fully mastered the principles of the art of slavery.

The tunnel by which the Brits sought to launch an attack against their German guards was never completed as the war ended before work on the tunnel could—but they never forgot the 50 fellow prisoners who sacrificed their lives. Freedom will prove a much greater challenge for, and extract a much larger toll from, North Koreans who, sadly, may not even yet know what it is they wish to fight for.

It is for this reason the Middle East's Arab Spring has little chance of reaching North Korea.

Programming a Robotic Mindset

In the world of robotics, programming is all important. Programmed to perform a single task, a robot then lacks the capability to perform a function outside of it. Any effort to issue a command for such an unauthorized task simply will not compute, leaving the task unaccomplished.

In discussions with lower level North Korean government representatives, when queried about subjects beyond which they have been programmed to talk, one almost senses a robot experiencing system overload. It becomes clear there is a line, necessitating an answer for creative or independent thought, over which the representative simply will not step.

In 1994, the author made the first of what would eventually be ten trips to North Korea—the last occurring in 2004. The first was with an international delegation composed of about two dozen private citizens or former government officials. Upon arrival, we were broken up into two-man groups, each given a government "handler/translator" who provided a guided tour of Pyongyang and the Demilitarized Zone (DMZ). We will call him "Mr. Pak."

For anyone familiar with what Pyongyang looked like at the end of hostilities in the Korean War in July 1953, the change is remarkable. Out of the ashes of ruin, a city—clearly built as a showcase—evolved. Long, straight and extremely wide boulevards leave the observer with the impression some roads were built for air rather than vehicular traffic. The streets appear to be able to handle massive volumes of traffic that simply does not exist as few vehicles are privately owned.

North Koreans are proud of their capital city—and rightly so. It was against this backdrop, Mr. Pak took us on a tour of an array of massive buildings and monuments. To each building and monument we were shown was attached am underlying theme attesting to the greatness of Kim Il Sung-who made it all possible.

Mr. Pak repeatedly hit this theme and other party lines as well during his discussions, all of which were clearly programmed presentations.

At one point, after taking us to a museum, he lectured how it was only North Korea that could boast it still possessed pure Korean culture. As South Korea, he explained, has been exposed to the West, its originally pure culture has been tainted by Western culture, giving rise to a hybrid one.

Later, we were taken to the DMZ—the Korean peninsula's equivalent to the "Berlin Wall" by which families as well as two nations remain separated. There, he lamented over the unnecessary divisiveness of this manmade barrier. Spewing forth an obviously well rehearsed dialogue, he suggested the North would like nothing more than to tear down the DMZ, allowing people from the South to freely travel to the North and vice-versa.

As guests of the North Korean government, we attentively and respectfully listened to Mr. Pak's "used car" salesman's pitches promoting the uniqueness of the North's culture and his country's longing for freedom of movement between bordering nations—movements not even tolerated within his own nation's borders. It was only when we broke for lunch, the author attempted to press him specifically on his comments.

Sitting at a table, three different bottles of soda were placed in front of us. Pointing at the first two, I asked

Mr. Pak the following: "If I opened these first two bottles and poured the contents into a single glass, will the contents of my glass differ from the contents in each individual bottle?"

With a quizzical look, Mr. Pak—unsure of where I was going—said, "Of course."

I then responded, "Now if the first bottle represents South Korean culture and the second Western culture, your point is the two have been mixed in my glass, tainting what was once true Korean culture, so that the South no longer can claim it is representative of it."

Regaining confidence, Mr. Pak responded, "Yes, that is exactly right."

I then queried, "If I then open this third bottle and pour the contents into my glass, will its contents differ from the contents of the third bottle?"

Again unsure of where this was going, Mr. Pak's quizzical look returned. He then responded, "Yes."

"Well," I continued, "if this third bottle represents North Korean culture—which you say is the only pure remaining Korean culture—and if the DMZ is removed—as you say you would like to see done so that people from the South could travel to the North and vice-versa—is it not true you would then have a culture in the North that no longer was representative of a true Korean culture? Wouldn't even North Korea's 'pure culture' disappear into the hybrid South Korea/Western culture mix you mentioned?"

Mr. Pak, with only a hint of a smile, tried to regain his composure. He then answered, "That is something we will talk about tomorrow."

Clearly, Mr. Pak had not been pre-briefed on how best to field such a question outside his programmed presentation and, as such, went into a default "does not compute" mode. It was clear too, he was unwilling to go out on a limb by making a statement not approved by his superiors. Unsurprisingly, the next day, there was no effort on his part to raise the issue with me again and, as a courtesy to him, I did not press the matter any further.

On a later trip, when the author queried a more senior North Korean official on a much more sensitive issue, he offered an answer which, although a little more creative, was totally non-responsive.

It was six months after Kim Il Sung's death and still unclear to outside observers exactly how Kim Jong Il's transition to power was progressing. While years had been spent prepping the North Korean people for Kim Jong Il's succession, there was no talk yet as to what the plan was for his succession in the event of an untimely demise. Accordingly, the senior North Korean official was queried on the issue of a succession to power. His response sought to quickly dismiss any further discussion of an issue verboten in his country. "The Dear Leader," he simply said, "is in very good health."

I immediately recognized, in a country where expressing the most innocent of opinions could prove deadly, his answer to the question could well have resulted in his execution. His subsequent cold stare ended any further effort on my part to obtain a responsive answer.

Putting Programmed Mind Control to Work for the Kim Dynasty

It is important to understand the capabilities given the Kim Dynasty by virtue of the power it wields over the minds of its people. A few examples exhibiting this capability in action and the results it can achieve are herein offered.

During the author's 1994 trip to North Korea, Pyongyang was bustling with activity—activity that became less apparent during subsequent trips. A few construction projects were in full swing. One was an engineering marvel—the Runga Suspension Bridge.

Hundreds of soldiers were observed struggling with cables, thousands of feet long, to suspend them above the 700 meter long bridge which, when completed, would extend across the Taedong River without the use of a single support member.

It was fascinating to watch the soldiers at work. The labor force was much larger than what one would anticipate as necessary—but that depended on what your job description was. There was much more manpower evident than there was machinery necessary to reduce the size of the work force. But among the workers were a large number of non-workers whose job was simply to serve as cheerleaders for those working.

As soldiers handled the cables, loudspeakers mounted on vehicles blared out patriotic music and songs in the background. A military band quietly stood at one end of the bridge, ready to take up the motivational beat upon command. As a song ended, a young female soldier would run up to the loudspeaker and exhort her fellow soldiers on to "victory" for "the Great Leader"—as Kim Il Sung was known. With flags and banners on the bridge blowing in the wind, the scene more resembled a football game than a construction project. But the message in the songs as well as the female soldier's exhortation was the same, "Thank you, Great Leader, for allowing us to serve you."

The industry, will and tenacity of the North Korean people—spurred on by similar exhortations—was best evidenced by a most remarkable engineering feat undertaken in 1981. The "West Sea Barrage," located 75 kilometers southwest of Pyongyang represented an engineering challenge of monumental proportion.

Already encumbered by mountainous terrain, North Korea is further hampered in achieving agricultural self-sufficiency by a limited fresh water supply in parts of the country. One such area included over 330,000 hectares of farmable land on the west coast of the country where the fresh water of the Taedong Rier flows into the salt waters of the West Sea. The result is a saline mixture which cannot be used for irrigation. To prevent the salinization of the river's fresh water, Kim Il Sung ordered a "barrage"—a barrier, dam and lock system almost five miles long at the mouth of the Taedong—be constructed.

Work began on the dam and lock portion of the system first. This was to stretch from the southern shore of the Taedong to a small island situated about two kilometers to the north. To begin the project, a temporary circular-shaped dam had to be constructed. The dam's function was to reclaim the land, 96 feet beneath the sea, that lay between these two points. After constructing the temporary dam and pumping out millions of metric tons of water, the muddy sea floor below was finally laid bare. But the mud did not provide the structural stability upon which to build the lock system's concrete foundation. Thus, workers found themselves having to remove all the mud in order to expose the rock bed underneath. This was a phenomenal task as the mud reached a depth of about 45 feet.

Once the southern portion of the barrage was eventually completed, the workers immediately went to work on constructing the longer northern segment. This involved erecting a wall of cement for a distance of 3.7 miles and to a depth of 96 feet. With 30,000 soldiers toiling both day and night, the barrage was completed in five years, requiring the use of over 1,100,000 tons of cement in the process.

Today, the West Sea Barrage operates as a living memorial to man's ability to overcome the challenges of nature. However, at the same time, one must question the wisdom of their leadership in undertaking such an enormous project when the same benefit could have been derived from a much less time consuming and costly solution, such as de-salinization plants. Accordingly, while serving as a living memorial to North Korean workers, the West Sea Barrage also serves as a memorial to a leadership's questionable judgment in seeking a more onerous solution where a more simplistic one would have sufficed.

While it is impossible to know what were Kim Il Sung's real motivations in ordering such a project to be undertaken, two reasons come to mind. First would be his desire to keep his military occupied—which such a five year project did. Kim Il Sung undoubtedly was concerned about a large military force being left idle to so reflect on the economic failures of juche. Second may well have been a motivation similar to that of the great pharaohs. Kim Il Sung may have sought to leave behind the equivalent of a North Korean "pyramid" by which future generations of North Koreans could marvel over his great accomplishments.

Yet another example of a controlled, and therefore disciplined, population was evident upon the occasion of Kim Il Sung's 82nd birthday on April 15, 1994. Thousands took to the streets and the city center to celebrate the event. What was remarkable was, despite the festivities that lasted long into the night, as the sun rose the next day, not a single piece of trash lay on the ground. Unlike the trash clean-up provided in the aftermath of far smaller crowds of celebrants in free societies, no such service was required in Pyongyang as celebrants were responsible for their own litter. One can only imagine what price is paid by a North Korean celebrant who fails to conduct himself in this manner.

The Deification Process Begins—and Goes Genetic

In 1859, the longest-serving US Marine Corps Commandant, Brig. General Archibald Henderson, died in office—the last 39 years of his 53-year military career spent residing in the Commandant's quarters in Washington, D.C.

Legend has it, after living in the home so long, Henderson forgot it belonged to the U.S. government—bequeathing it to his family. Lacking legal title to the home, however, he was unable to do so.

As the most senior leader of Marines at that time, Henderson's position entitled him to reside in the quarters. But after nearly four decades, the longevity of his service clouded his memory, causing him to believe he owned an entitlement he did not. Ownership remained with the US government.

Where totalitarianism reigns, a similar sense of entitlement arises. But there is one major difference between the entitlement Henderson believed was his and that of a totalitarian leader: While the former's sense of entitlement was innocently derived, the latter's is not.

Few totalitarian leaders, outside of those whose power derives from royal bloodlines, have been so influenced by their sense of entitlement to believe they can pass their authority over a nation's people down to their own issue. Where such thoughts have flickered, they have quickly been snuffed out.

For Kim Il Sung, this was not the case. He possessed a strong sense of entitlement to authoritarian rule. Perhaps because he began it as the leader of a new nation—one having no history in place to prevent his exercising such an entitlement—he sought to establish a family dynasty, eventually easing his people into accepting one family rule. As they had already willingly accepted him as a deity, Kim Il Sung knew a genetic succession would play well in North Korea. Kim Il Sung's deification process started soon after he came to power in 1948, courtesy of the Soviets. As one Russian official later wrote, Kim Il Sung essentially was "created from zero"—pitched as a hero who had joined the resistance against Japan, creating at age 19 a battle-ready army, single-handedly driving the Japanese out of the country. Contributing to Kim Il Song's image were efforts by Hwang Jong Yop (the 1997 defector mentioned earlier) to distance Kim Il Sung from his Soviet protégé, Josef Stalin, by re-writing historical references to him, making it appear as if Kim Il Sung had been the original founder of the Worker's Party of Korea—which he had not. Kim Il Sung's cult personality continued to develop up through his death in 1994 and continues even after his death today.

Kim Jong Il's cult legacy attached soon after his birth. A book later written in North Korea and chronicling his life credited him as a young child with bravely pointing out a spy to authorities when others feared speaking out and then disappearing into the crowd suggesting a hint of humility. Born, not in a manger, but supposedly atop a sacred mountain—Mount Paektu—his birth was heralded, not by a heavenly star, but a double rainbow. On occasion, the comments further exaggerating Kim Jong Il's cult image have reached ridiculous proportions, such as claims, after taking up golf, he shot several holes-in-one during his first game.

The North Korean media could probably give Hollywood fiction scriptwriters a run for their money for the positive light in which they constantly portrayed, first, Kim Il Sung, and later Kim Jong Il. Both were touted for their insightful visits to industrial plants to impart their wisdom on how to improve factory performance. Yet, after having imparted such wisdom during a combined 63 years of family rule, no one seems to question why the economy remains in shambles.

Domestic news sources recently drew the picture of a Kim Jong Il dedicated to his people, journeying around the country to share his "field guidance with patriotic devotion despite the biting cold...(working)...hard day and night, having uncomfortable sleep and taking rice-balls" while serving his nation. "Seeing his dedication," the news account continued, "in tears, the people would ask him to stop making any more journeys along snow-covered roads in cold weather and sitting up all night."

This picture was quite a contrast to the opulent lifestyle the "Dear Leader," as he was known, really enjoyed. His evening parties—some lasting days—involved eating, drinking and sex binges that would have caused Hugh Hefner to blush. No wonder he passed away at age 69 of further heart complications following a 2008 stroke, having compressed several decades of wild living into the few remaining years of his life.

An ever hopeful North Korean media editorialized in the days after Dear Leader's December 17th death that a "spring of prosperity under socialism will surely come to the country thanks to the patriotic devotion of Kim Jong Il who blocked the howling wind of history till the last moments of his life." One can only wonder how many North Koreans fail to grasp the only thing their leader blocked while alive was a better life for his people. Apparently, as observed by some "non-mourning" mourners at his December 28th funeral, not all North Koreans were Kim Jong Il cult worshippers.

But the deification process works. On one trip to North Korea years after Kim Il Sung's death, the author was taken to the Kumsusan Mausoleum where the father rests embalmed in Lenin-esque repose. Not even the passage of time had dampened the grief of North

Koreans streaming in by the thousands to view the remains of the "Great Leader."

For those aware of Kim Il Sung's sins, the wails and cries of mourners are surreal, for those sins inflicted so much suffering upon his people. However, the combination of limited information flow and deification placed him on such a high pedestal, his public failed to see him for the brutal leader he really was. Similarly, the sins of Kim Jong Il remained invisible to another generation who viewed their Dear Leader through rose-colored glasses. Now another generation awaits the royal reign of the "Young Master," as Kim Jong Un was called by his father.

Other monikers seem to be in the running for Kim Jong Un as "The Great Successor" and the "Supreme Leader" as the country's media has dubbed him. In a surprising reference in a news release by the National Defense Commission dated December 30th, he was called the "Supreme Commander" of the 1.2 million strong North Korean army—a title bestowed upon his father, Kim Jong Il during his lifetime.

The deification process has already begun for Kim Jong Un. On the occasion of his January 8th birthday, a Chinese magazine ran an article about him provided by North Korean sources. It claims he learned to drive at the age of three and five years later was able to drive a car at the speed of 75 miles per hour. Although he is known not to have had any military training, the North Korean media now claims at the age of 16 he wrote his first thesis on military strategy after only three to four hours of sleep at night and going without meals to study.

Kim Jong Un now conducts visits to army bases where, much like was done for his father in the early days of his rule, each military unit tries to outdo the others by bestowing the greatest gifts or honors upon him. A North Korean produced documentary aired on his birthday quoted military leaders as saying, "The respected comrade Kim Jong-un is perfectly versed in all military strategies and... displays excellent military leadership." Much like little children excited over the arrival of Santa Clause, footage of Kim Jong Un visiting their base had soldiers jumping for joy. Describing him as "the spitting image" of his father and grandfather in personality and leadership, the documentary labelled him as "the genius among the geniuses" in military knowledge.

Just like the February 16th birthday of Kim Jong Il and the April 15th birthday of Kim Il Sung were made important holidays with special events scheduled in celebration, so too can we expect Kim Jong Un's January 8th birthday to be similarly celebrated as the new leader settles in on his throne.

As the North's propaganda machine spits out tribute after tribute, it becomes clear, just as Muslims today continue to revere Prophet Muhammad and his heirs, so too do North Koreans continue to revere Kim Il Sung and his.

An Attempt to Mirror Kim Il Sung's "Cult Persona" and Juche Idea Outside North Korea's Borders: The Romanian Experiment

Westerners can only shake their heads in disbelief at the success the Kim dynasty has had in convincing their people to make great personal sacrifices on behalf of their leadership. Taking liberties with a line from Winston Churchill's famous World War II speech about the Royal Air Force, "Never before was so much sacrificed by so many for so few." How Kim Il Sung was able to cast millions of his countrymen under such a spell—one still remaining intact today—is difficult to comprehend. And, on at least one occasion, the magic proved spell-bounding beyond the borders of North Korea.

Almost a quarter century after Kim Il Sung came to power, he was visited by another world leader—Romanian leader Nicolae Ceausescu. Having come to power through the country's Communist Party in 1965, Ceausescu was viewed as a reformed communist, eager to ease control over his people. His desire for greater rights for his people, however, would give way to a sinister motivation to brutally control them after a 1971 trip to North Korea.

On this trip, Ceausescu visited China, North Vietnam, Mongolia and North Korea. He was accompanied by the Secretary of the Communist Party Central Committee, Ion Iliescu, who years later would serve as the country's first democratically elected president. Iliescu reported that what Ceausescu saw in North Korea mesmerized the Romanian leader as he became "literally fascinated by Korea. Much more (so) than by China where an environment of disorder characteristic of the cultural revolution was prevailing. North Korea was the perfect model of an absolute totalitarianism."

So impressed was Ceausescu that upon his return to Bucharest, Iliescu went on to explain, "he drew up a kind of platform for a cultural revolution Romanian style." Having taken note of Kim Il Sung's success in creating a personality cult—and the more limited success of Mao Zedong in China—Ceausescu embarked upon a similar course to build his own cult following. To assist the effort, books on juche were translated into Romanian and widely distributed.

But, the North Korean leader must have engaged a much more effective propagandist to sell his cult persona to his people than Ceausescu did to sell it to his. Kim Il Sung's rule would last until he was struck down by a heart attack in 1994. Ceausescu would not enjoy such longevity or such tolerance by his people. In 1989, a revolution ended his rule. After trying to escape, he and his wife were captured. Following a hasty trial, both were executed on Christmas Day by firing squad.

While Ceausescu led his crusade to mirror the North Korean model of "absolute totalitarianism," enjoying life at the great sacrifice of his people, his effort to do so—like Romania's economy—was a fiasco. It raises the question as to why Kim Il Sung's crusade succeeded while Ceausescu's did not. The answer may lie in where both men started their rule—and yet another insight into North Koreans' tolerance of a brutal regime.

Ceausescu was Romania's second Communist Party leader. He had come to power in 1965 after the death of his predecessor, Gheorghe Gheorghiu-Dej, whose reign had started in 1948. A Stalinist, Gheorghiu-Dej was also a nationalist who very adeptly was able to maneuver Romania outside the sphere of complete Soviet influence that hindered the economies of other Eastern European countries. His breakout from that sphere came with the death of Soviet leader Josef Stalin in 1952. He embarked upon a semi-autonomous foreign and domestic economic policy that brought with it greater freedoms for Romanians.

In 1965, Gheorghiu-Dej died of lung cancer. (It was later learned his death was expedited by his medical treatment in Moscow where doctors were instructed to irradiate him for defying Soviet rule.) A conflict between the two leading contenders for power in Romania to succeed him resulted in Ceausescu's selection as a compromise candidate. To the Soviet's dismay, however, Ceausescu continued Gheroghiu-Dej's semi-independent policies.

Because of this post-World War II evolution of independence from Soviet control, Romanians enjoyed greater freedoms than the rest of their Soviet Bloc neighbors. But this abruptly changed for them after

Ceausescu's trip to North Korea and the launch of his cult persona initiative.

It is interesting to compare this situation in Romania to that which existed in North Korea in 1948 when Kim Il Sung came to power. As the Soviets preached to the North Korean people, they had—allegedly along with Kim Il Sung's participation—driven the Japanese out of the country at the end of World War II, ending their very brutal rule. During that occupation, the Japanese had endeavored to eradicate Korean culture and replace it with their own. The defeat of Japan left Koreans in the north euphoric as any rule—even, initially, that of the Soviets and later of Kim Il Sung—was better than Japanese rule.

The difference was that the rule North Koreans experienced under Kim Il Sung, as bad as it was, still represented a step up from that experienced under the Japanese. After all, under the Soviets and Kim Il Sung they retained their culture. A Korean leader had come to power to repair the peoples' broken national spirit, replacing it with one of pride and patriotism. Kim Il Sung provided his people with a sense of accomplishment and restored their personal dignity. A charismatic leader, Kim Il Sung convinced them they could control their own destiny by collectively working for the common good. Today, that attitude permeates every aspect of North Korea's culture—from its music to its dance to its literature.

While conditions were right for Kim Il Sung's initiative, they were not for Ceausescu's. The rights and liberties Romanians enjoyed at the beginning of Ceausescu's rule were extinguished after 1971. Ceausescu took Romanians in a direction that represented a step down to Kim Il Sung's step up.

In conducting his laboratory experiment in mind control, Kim Il Sung had the benefit of being perceived by his people in a positive light while Ceausescu was perceived by his in a negative one. While Kim Il Sung was therefore able to move forward quickly in planting the seeds of juche and his personality cult, Ceausescu met immediate resistance in Romania—resistance which ultimately manifested itself in the form of the 1989 revolution that buried the juche idea, as far as Romanians were concerned, forever.

Disruption of "Rule by Kim" Unlikely

So, how important is the Kim personality cult to a stable transition of power in North Korea? It is absolutely critical. Should the chain of the family's succession be broken by a renegade general or any non-Kim family member, a question of legitimacy would arise from among the people. The only rule North Koreans have known in their nation's 63 year history is "rule by Kim." Thus, how goes the Kim dynasty also goes the country's elite. As former US special envoy to North Korea Stephen Bosworth aptly puts it, the "regime is in a classic 'we all hang together or we all hang separately.'" It is, he says, "a great imperative for cohesion." Another North Korean expert adds concerning the country's elite, "All have a vested interest in regime survival (to which) their own personal safety and survival is inextricably tied."

Past Power Plays—Son Proves Unlike Father

There is one aspect of maintaining power in North Korea where Kim Jong Un's grandfather proved very adept but his father did not. Kim Il Sung maintained a delicate balance between the country's two main power bases—the Party and the military. He feared the consequences of allowing one to garner too much authority over the other. But, coming to power in 1994, Kim Jong Il threw his lot in with the army, as evidenced by his "military first" policy and his promotion to general rank of more officers in the first decade of his rule than Kim Il Sung promoted in the 46 years of his. Allowing such a power base shift has undoubtedly influenced such aggressive acts by Pyongyang like last year's torpedoing of the South Korean destroyer "Cheonan."

Despite 20 years of preparation Kim Jong Il had before assuming power at age 52, the military was soon able to influence his decision-making. At age 27, with less than ten percent of the preparation time and despite his recent overnight promotion to four-star general status,

Kim Jong Un will prove far more malleable by his military handlers.

Military Influence Bodes Well for Stable Transition but not for a Stable Peninsula as Evidenced by "Generals Gone Wild"

There are several indicators the military influence is already taking root. It may well be what prompted Pyongyang's saber-rattling test-firing of a missile only two days after Kim Jong Il's death, possibly meant as a warning to outsiders. It is also indicated by North Korean media reports Kim Jong Un would inherit his father's "*sungun*" (military first) policy. And, Jang Sung-Taek, an uncle of the new leader who started gaining prominence after Kim Jong Il's 2008 stroke and recovery, was observed wearing a general's uniform soon after the Dear Leader's death. (Jang is the husband of Kim Jong Il's younger sister, Kim Kyong Hui, whose appearance at the December 29 memorial service for the Dear Leader suggests she too holds influence.)

Senior generals recognize their power is clearly linked to a smooth transition to Kim Jong Un whom, they full expect, to continue with his father's "military first" policy. Accordingly, they will ensure they position themselves to cast the same mold for "The Great Successor" as was cast for "The Dear Leader." But the stability of the North's power transition belies the inherent danger that such military influence wields. It most certainly has proven to be a factor in the North's numerous provocations against the South which have generated periodic instability on the peninsula during Kim Jong Il's rule.

A recent case in point of "generals gone wild" may well be the cowardly attack on the South Korean frigate "Cheonan" in March 2010. It is reported Pyongyang's torpedoing and sinking of the ship, which led to the deaths of 46 South Korean sailors, was ordered by four-star North Korean General Kim Myong-guk under whose command the navy fell. The general had fallen out of favor with Kim Jong Il due to a November 2009 North/South sea confrontation generating a result in which Pyongyang was thoroughly humiliated. It resulted in the general being stripped of a star. In an effort to regain face, he then masterminded the Cheonan attack. Its successful outcome for Pyongyang apparently regained the lost star for General Kim as a photograph of him after the March 2010 sinking revealed he again was wearing a fourth star.

Post-Funeral Power Analysis—Some Mourners May No Longer be Buying Into the Kim Cult But Will They Ever Pull Back the Curtain Exposing North Korea's "Wizards of Oz" for What They Really Are?

The emergence in 2008 of Kim Jong Un's uncle Jang Sung-Taek represented a concerted effort by Kim Jong

Il to preserve the family dynasty. While Kim Jong Un will not—at least initially—have anything near the authority his father and grandfather enjoyed, three centers of influence will be in play trying to manipulate Kim Jong Un's march to power. These include the Party, the army and his family. The first indication as to whom has the inside track and who does not played out at the Dear Leader's funeral.

On the outside due to their absence from the funeral procession are Kim Jong Un's two older brothers.

Joining Jang as a top person of influence is Ri Yong Ho, who heads the North Korean military's General Staff. Like Jang, Ri also emerged from the shadows in the aftermath of Kim Jong Il's stroke. Both had prominent positions at the funeral. As Jang walked just behind Kim Jong Un on one side of the hearse followed by senior Party leaders, Ri led a group of senior generals and the defense minister on the other.

The street was lined with both civilians and military personnel who continuously wailed during the three hour procession. The mourners flailed their hands, beat their chests and stomped their feet (unknown is whether their actions were motivated by emotion or the bitter cold and snow that fell earlier). In continuing the cult persona of Kim Jong Il, North Korean commentators attributed the snowfall to "heaven's grief" over the Dear Leader's loss.

Interesting to observe were mourners closest to the street that seemed to manifest an intensity of grief not exhibited by those standing further back. Obviously from reviewing film footage it is difficult to determine whether their absence of emotion was representative of a group who was no longer "buying in" to the Kim cult persona or simply represented stoicism. Perhaps their empty bellies served as a great motivator to awaken them to the realities of a leadership's failure to fulfill its responsibilities to them. As isolated as the people of the Hermit Kingdom are, however, one can only wonder if they will ever have the capability to pull back the curtain behind which the Kim dynasty hides exposing Pyongyang's "Wizards of Oz" for what they really are. A faint glimmer of the people's willingness to voice their frustrations against their government actually occurred in 2009 after an economic decision caused families to lose their life savings (discussed below)—but, again, due to an inability to organize, the effort was quickly snuffed out.

"Old Guard" to be Replaced by More of the Same Plus Other Indicators of How Goes the Transition

As far as military and Party leaders are concerned, it will be interesting to see if Kim Jong Un opts to stay with the aging leaders in place, promoted by his father, or will decide to replace this "old guard" with a younger breed who would then owe him their personal allegiance. Because of the lengthy time period Kim Jong Il served as "leader-in-waiting" before his father died, he was able to influence some promotions before taking power, thus easing his transition. With a much shorter "leader-in-waiting" period, Kim Jong Un was unable to play such a role before his father's death thrust him onto the throne. But when he does start replacing senior officials, he will probably choose to do so with their sons/daughters or other direct blood relatives so as to make the replacement effort more palatable to the old guard.

There will be some near term indicators as to how the transition is progressing. An increase at the country's labor camps will suggest a purge is in the works. Another will be the actions of various members of the country's elite. Some, fearing a purge is or will be mounted, will seek to defect. This fear may already be in play based on the actions of some North Korean officials stationed in Beijing who, having been summoned home, are dragging their feet in doing so. Perhaps anticipating such a possible exodus from North Korea, Pyongyang has already tightened border controls.

But the influence centers all understand the march to power must be taken with Kim Jong Un—not without him—as regime survival is critical to any single influence center. Therefore, the speed of the march will depend on how quick a study Kim Jong Un is in mastering his ability to drive a North Korean power machine that in the past has been fueled on brutality. This march was started before Kim Jong Il's death, as perceived opponents to his son's future rule were incarcerated in labor camps and army officers suspected of not fully supporting Kim Jong Un's four-star rise to power were demoted. If Kim Jong Un is taken out of the picture by any one influence center, all bets are off as to the country's future stability.

Kim Jong Un's Baggage Doesn't Slow Down His Transition

With all eyes focused on Kim Jong Un, there are rumors he comes to power with some political baggage. Allegedly, he played a role in the country's 2009 decision to revalue its currency—an action that further hardened life for the people as their life savings were almost wiped out. To avoid linkage to his son, Kim Jong Il held his finance minister responsible, executing him in April 2011.

The day after Kim Jong Il's funeral and at his December 29 memorial service, this baggage did not appear to inhibit support by the country's king makers who, for the first time, publicly declared Kim Jong Un their "Supreme Leader." Another indicator that various influence centers are unified in their support is the accumulation of the numerous titles Kim Jong Un will need to establish both his credentials and legitimacy as head of state—marking collective acceptance by the influence centers of the Kim family's royal lineage. This further suggests the path to transition will be a smooth one.

While the throne appears to be Kim Jong Un's, it will be how he starts to wield his power that will determine to what extent he ultimately succeeds in fully exercising those powers. But, for the moment, it is clear events unfolding in North Korea seem to be in line with Kim Jong Il's wishes. As a South Korean analyst suggests, "Kim Jong Il laid a red silk carpet and Kim Jong Un only needs to walk on it."

Will "The Great Successor" Cut a Path as His "Own Man" or Follow His "Old Man?"

It will be interesting to see too how Kim Jong Un chooses to establish himself. Will he sit back and allow others to blaze that trail for him or will he feel a need to do it himself, demonstrating an effort to become his own man? In looking for distinctions between father and son and, if hairstyle is any indicator of what is to come, Kim Jong Un's closely-shorn hair at least represents a contrast to the bouffant hairstyle of his father.

As his father proved effective, Kim Jong Un will be quickly schooled in how to play the West and South Korea to meet the North's most overriding needs. As diminished food supplies continue to be a problem for Pyongyang, we will see an encouraging message or two from the North that they are open to talks and negotiations. We can count on food and/or oil shipments to them as an enticement to further open the door.

An early indicator this card will be played is Pyongyang's New Year's message for 2012 which was devoid of the usual anti-US rhetoric, silent on its often self-praised nuclear program and provided a hint of continuing discussions. It openly admits "the food problem is a burning issue." But never failing to give its own people false hopes, the message boasts that the country is "at the epochal point to open the gates of a thriving country." The Hollywood fiction scriptwriting continues.

As the influence centers look to sort out their relationships with Kim Jong Un, the new leader will be determining which of them provides him with the greatest comfort level. At this point, based on the relationships his father had to sort out, the military and his family will be at the front of the influence pack.

Having witnessed how Kim Jong Il and the military worked together to increase international tensions, it would not be surprising to see Kim Jong Un embark upon a similar course. He has seen strength and brutality as leadership characteristics the power machine rewards. But, while such a role may endear him to the military, it also runs the risk of bringing the peninsula into conflict as a young, inexperienced leader with access to the fourth largest army in the world decides to follow in his father's footsteps.

In Looking to Kim Jong Un's Transition, It is Important to Understand the Path his Father Chose During his Journey to Power

When Kim Il Sung—a man who ruled with an iron fist—died, Kim Jong Il initially was content to remain within his late father's shadow. As he began to feel more secure in a leadership role, he eventually stepped into the limelight to cut his own path, which caused him to develop his military first policy. But he did not altogether abandon the policies his father established. Aggressive acts against South Korea by the North were a constant theme in Pyongyang's foreign policy.

Just like Kim Il Sung embraced a policy of confrontation aimed south of the border including the kidnapping of foreign citizens, sending a special operations team into South Korea to assassinate its president (killing its First Lady in the process), tunneling under South Korea's border from the North in order to provide North Korean invasion forces with access south of the DMZ in the event of war, blowing up a South Korean passenger plane, etc., Kim Jung Il followed suit with mini-submarine incursions into South Korean waters, sending spies into the South, torpedoing a South Korean destroyer, conducting an artillery attack against a South Korean island, assassinating South Korean citizens, etc.

The military's early influence over Kim Jong Un is indicated by what was his first official visit of 2011. Just as Kim Jong Il regularly visited army units, Kim Jong Un made his first field inspection on December 30th. In so doing, and demonstrating his inexperience at how best to praise the military forces he now commands, he simply praised them for closely watching enemy troops. Clearly lacking oratorical skills apparently does not inhibit one's rise when one is a Kim.

It must be kept in mind as one reads through the above list of unprovoked acts of aggression that violence and confrontation is an often-used tool for dictators seeking to take the focus of the people off domestic problems and directing it to international ones. And, if that international incident or outside threat fails to present itself, then the dictator must create the outside threat himself. Chances are, therefore, Kim Jong Un will pursue the latter by continuing a foreign policy aimed at creating conflict with the South.

In a Land Where the Sun Don't Shine, North Korea Uses South Korea's "Sunshine Policy" to Rain Down on Seoul's Parade for Better Relations

Of note in this regard is that not even a decade of appeasement by South Korea during Kim Jong Il's 17 year rule sufficed to quell Pyongyang's appetite for violence and determination to arm itself with a nuclear weapon. The South launched its "Sunshine" foreign policy towards the North which sought to avoid confrontation at all costs. Two members of South Korea's liberal party nurtured the policy as president.

Begun in 1998 by South Korean President Kim Dae Jung and continued by his successor, President Roh Moo Hyun, the policy involved a South Korean declaration that it had no intention of absorbing the North or undermining its government.

The policy's name was taken from an Aesop fable, "The North Wind and the Sun," in which the sun and the wind compete to cause a man to take his coat off. Although giving rise to the 2000 summit meeting between Kim Dae Jung and Kim Jong Il in Pyongyang, the policy turned out to pretty much be a fable for Seoul as Pyongyang used it time and time again to extract aid from the South while giving up little in return.

Kim Jong Il would not even honor his promise to hold a second summit in Seoul, forcing President Roh to come to Pyongyang in 2007 for a second meeting to take place. It was a classic Kim Jong Il mindset of, "if the mountain won't come to Mohammad then Mohammad must come to the mountain," an analogy in which the Dear Leader envisioned himself as "the mountain." The fact Kim Jong Il refused to go to Seoul increased his stature within the army. But the Sunshine Policy's absolute failure to move Pyongyang off its aggressive course ultimately caused President Roh's conservative successor, Lee Myung Bak, to fully abandon it.

Pyongyang's history of aggression appears to be a "badge of honor" for the Kim family in demonstrating strong leadership to their followers. We shall eventually know whether Kim Jong Un will opt to continue

Pyongyang's policy of aggression—in existence since the end of the Korean war--or to pursue one of true rapprochement. But, as previously suggested, the Kim family's DNA is strongly on the side of the former.

In a contrast to Pyongyang's New Year's message avoiding anti-US rhetoric, there was definitely no sign of a softening of its position towards South Korea evident in a December 30th statement released by the powerful National Defense Committee—one containing only a hint of anti-Americanism. It declared North Korea will never negotiate with current South Korean President Lee Myung Bak—a position most likely taken due to Pyongyang's continuing anger that Lee abandoned the Sunshine Policy upon taking office in 2008. It went on to make clear to both South Korea and the US its new leadership does not want to signal any change is in the wind for Pyongyang, claiming: "We declare solemnly and confidently that the foolish politicians around the world, including the puppet group in South Korea, should not expect any change from us. We will never deal with the traitor group of Lee Myung Bak."

As suggested earlier, whether such a harsh statement coming so quickly after Kim Jong Un's coronation accurately portrays Pyongyang's true position or is simply a play-it-tough-now tactic to wrangle greater concessions from Seoul later remains to be seen. The latter may be a ploy as indicated by the statement's continuation that Pyongyang "will continue to push hard toward the path of improved relations" (although based upon the North's past performance, it is difficult to believe it has even embarked upon such a path yet).

Kim Jong Un Will Play the Intimidation Card to Measure South Koreans' National Morality

In trying to understand how Kim Jong Un will play off his father's policy towards South Korea, it is important first to understand how the South has effectively been played over the last dozen years by Pyongyang's efforts to intimidate.

William Shakespeare wrote a 17th century play posing a question he then left unanswered: "Can one desire too much of a good thing?" In dealing with a long history of North Korean aggression over the past several years, the South Koreans have provided their answer to this question by ballot.

South Koreans voted the Grand National Party (GNP) out of office in 1998 and opposition leader Kim Dae Jung into office as president in 1999. It was President Kim who first launched the conciliatory policy towards North Korea known as the Sunshine Policy. The policy was continued by Kim's successor in office, Roh Moo Hyun. But ten years of appeasement did nothing to alter Pyongyang's course of aggression against the South.

Seoul's appeasement policy has been a one-way street to the North, only benefitting Pyongyang with shipments of food and oil—as well as cash paid to entice the North to hold two summit conferences generating international attention but no substantive results. Meanwhile, the benefit to the South has been nil. Accordingly, voters returned the GNP to power in 2009, electing Lee Myung Bak as president.

Lee immediately abandoned the Sunshine Policy. With a conservative government in office, it appeared South Koreans had finally had their fill of aggression by their neighbor to the North, registering their preference for a leader who would take action against Pyongyang in the event of a future act of violence.

If anything should have sparked a desire for action by the South Koreans to retaliate against the North, it should have been Pyongyang's March 26, 2010 torpedoing of the destroyer Cheonan, which claimed 46 South Korean lives. It failed to do so as South Koreans continued to demonstrate a preference for inaction in the face of unabashed aggression.

On May 20, 2010—the same day the results of an investigation conducted by international experts into the cause of the sinking were released, holding the North responsible—South Korean politicians vying for 4000 offices in local and regional elections started their campaigns. President Lee condemned the North for the attack, vowing it "will pay a price" for its most recent—and most egregious—act of aggression. He made clear inaction was no longer an acceptable foreign policy in dealing with North Korea.

It was anticipated, therefore, out of the 16 races taking place in South Korea that were considered critical (i.e., involving major city mayor and provincial governor positions) and with anti-North sentiment running high, the GNP would sweep nine of them. With the greatest turnout in 15 years, voters sent a clear message to Seoul. Having to choose between standing up to such aggression or continuing to enjoy the good life, voters opted for the latter. Out of the 16 races, the GNP only took six.

Having enjoyed "too much of a good thing" for too long, South Koreans showed they had no taste for war, no matter how egregious the North's act was. Instead of embracing the Cheonan as a "Pearl Harbor" moment, voters even chose to blame their own government—accusing it of having rigged the Cheonan investigation and "provoked" the North by abandoning the Sunshine Policy!

Most indicative of continuing tolerance by the South of the North's belligerence came from the South Korea's eastern province of Gangwon—a long-time GNP stronghold. Situated along the border with North Korea, Gangwon—in the event of war—would be prime battlefield real estate. For the first time in 16 years, the GNP lost the province in an election.

While Lee had never threatened war but had stated he would seek UN action, opposition politicians claimed the GNP's election drubbing called for the president to "abandon his confrontational policy on North Korea and ease tensions on the Korean peninsula." Some politicians went further, demanding he apologize to the North for having turned the Cheonan's loss into an unnecessary national security crisis. Ironically, a North Korean act of aggression had so intimidated South Koreans focused on avoiding war at all costs, they created an anti-Lee regime bandwagon that Pyongyang also quickly joined. Feeling its oats, Pyongyang announced it was satisfied with the election results and then warned it may retaliate against Seoul for its "intolerable" campaign to punish North Korea through the UN.

A deciding factor in the elections was the high percentage of young South Koreans who supported the opposition party. Rather than feel any sense of moral obligation to punish the North for the deaths of 46 of their countrymen, these voters—not wanting to give up the good life—decided taking the moral high road posed too much personal risk and sacrifice on their part. The election results tempered President Lee who, a few days later, announced—while still blaming the North for the ship's loss—there was absolutely no possibility of war.

Kim Jong Un can be counted on to play the intimidation card to influence the South's behavior. Knowing the North's intimidation of the South provides him with the upper hand—one he can credit to his father's belligerent policy toward Seoul—Kim Jong Un knows, so far, South Korea lacks the willingness to draw a line in the sand which it would then steadfastly defend. Thus, Kim Jong

Un has no reason to allow Seoul to dictate how their relationship evolves under his leadership.

Kim Jong Il did a good job in breaking the will of the South Korean people to believe in fighting for that which should be valued most—human life; Kim Jong Un will now be coached by his advisors to test that lack of will.

With the animosity the North harbors for President Lee's actions in cutting off their "gravy train" under the Sunshine Policy, it will seek to influence the next presidential election in South Korea in the same manner it did South Korea's 2010 local elections. It will look to influence voters to elect a more Pyongyang-friendly president who will help feed its people so Pyongyang can concentrate on its on-again/off-again nuclear program: on when it desperately needs aid; off when it does not or just doesn't care. Halting its nuclear program temporarily for food and oil, however, is a well-traveled road for the North as it has proven quite fruitful.

It is undoubtedly discouraging to those allies who fought in the Korean War 62 years ago, coming to Seoul's defense after it was invaded by the North, to witness the unwillingness of the South Korean people to stand tall against Pyongyang's bullying. Six plus decades of peace on the peninsula has immensely improved life for its citizens but, unfortunately, it has de-sensitized its youth to the realization sometimes personal sacrifice is necessary when tyrants strike out. The good life has left the South Korean people desiring too much of a good thing. Such a life has so morally disoriented them; they choose to allow themselves to be intimidated by the beast of tyranny rather than to slay it.

Once before in history, democratic states—intimidated by tyranny—chose to cower from rather than challenge it. In the years prior to World War II, President Franklin Delano Roosevelt reminded them, "There must be recognition of the fact that national morality is as vital as private morality." In the years ahead, South Koreans can count on the new North Korean leader-in-training to intimidate them further in an effort to assess whether they possess either.

Ensuring No One Gets a Bigger Share of Pie!

The border separating North Korea's population of 23 million and South Korea's 49 million is the DMZ—considered the most heavily defended border in the world. Although the South has more than twice the population of the North, it is the North with its 1.1 million man army that enjoys almost a 2-to-1 advantage in military forces. It is also at the DMZ that the political gamesmanship played between these two nations almost reaches—at least to foreign observers though probably not to the Koreans involved—comical proportions.

The DMZ stretches 250 kilometers east/west across the Korean peninsula, along the 38th Parallel North and through the historic town of Panmunjom. A buffer zone about 2.5 miles wide between the two Koreas, the DMZ is a product of the Korean conflict—a war initiated by the North's leadership. (It was not until the late 1990's, however, after Soviet archives were made public following the fall of the Soviet Union, we learned Kim Il Sung was acting on Stalin's orders.) While the small village of Panmunjom serves to symbolize the wounds of division caused by that war, it is the DMZ that serves to keep the two Koreas—and a single people—separated.

Approaching the building where the armistice ending the Korean war was signed, one has an opportunity to scan the surrounding area. The rice fields there and the workers laboring in them belie the tensions that existed then and continue now along this political fault line where soldiers on either side stand ready to answer a clarion call to war. (Note: While an Armistice Agreement was signed on July 27, 1953, a peace treaty never was. The belligerents agreed to the DMZ demarcation, which both sides have patrolled ever since.)

The room where the agreement was signed remains unchanged from what it looked like decades earlier. It originally contained just two large tables and chairs for the negotiators; however, a third, smaller table had to be added during negotiations for reasons bordering on absurdity, although it is most telling about the deep animosity the two nations shared then and continue to share today for each other.

During the 1953 negotiations, with representatives from the South sitting at one large table and from the North at the other, a deadlock was reached when one side refused to accept a document for review being handed over by the other side—as long as the document physically remained within the tendering party's hands. Therefore, a third table was brought in so that the document could be placed on it by the tendering party and, once physically released, the receiving party could then pick it up, thereby avoiding any direct physical contact between them.

Negotiations today are conducted at a different location, in a single-room building. There are actually three buildings, running parallel to each other and perpendicular to the 38th Parallel North that straddle the Korean border. Exactly half of each building is situated on the North and half on the South side. Inside the center building is a single table, positioned in a similar manner, straddling the border. The exact same number of chairs is found on both sides. Atop the table are an equal number of microphones for each side. One side of the building always remains an exact mirror image of the other. As one takes this all in, one cannot help but envision the North and South as children—each determined that the other will not receive a bigger portion of the pie.

One can enter these buildings from their respective North/South ends, which remain guarded at all times. While visitors are allowed inside, they must exit through the same door through which they entered. Thus, within the confines of the building they entered, visitors can freely move back and forth across the border.

Supposedly, a major sore point for the North at the DMZ was the construction by the South of a concrete wall, several meters high, stretching for as far as the eye can see. Clearly visible from the North, it is hidden from the view of an observer standing on the South side due to the vegetation that conceals it. The North claims it is this wall that inhibits free passage of Koreans on either side of it from transiting the border. Additionally, and surrealistically, the North claims it has a negative environmental impact—a position difficult for outsiders to accept based on

Pyongyang's disregard for the welfare of its own people. Because the wall remains "invisible" from the South, when representatives of the North raise the issue of the concrete barrier, the South's response is to plead ignorance, responding "What wall?"

The Road Down Under

On November 15, 1974, North and South Korean relations hit a new low.

A South Korean reconnaissance unit, patrolling the western sector of the DMZ, on its side of the barrier near Gorang-po, noticed something unusual. Steam was observed rising out of the ground. Closer examination determined the steam was the result of underground digging activity. The activity was coming from North Korea, under the DMZ, toward the South. A tunnel was obviously being excavated, estimated to be at a depth of 145 feet.

The South Koreans dug a tunnel of their own to intercept the North Korean tunnel. As the South Koreans broke through, they were taken under fire by the North Koreans. An initial attempt to examine the tunnel ended in the deaths of a US Navy and South Korean Marine Corps officer who had tripped an explosive device set by the North Koreans as a booby trap.

Once the South Koreans were able to safely access the tunnel, they were amazed at the enormity of the task undertaken by the North Koreans. The tunnel was four feet high and three feet wide. Its walls and ceiling were reinforced with cement. The tunnel was large enough to run an entire infantry regiment through every hour. It was equipped with 60-watt lamps and 220-volt power lines, a narrow gauge railway and rail cars. The estimated length of the tunnel was 3700 yards, of which roughly one-third extended beyond North Korea's border into the South. There were sleeping and weapons storage areas carved out as well.

If completed, the tunnel would have provided invading North Korean forces entry into the South less than 65 kilometers from Seoul. More importantly, it would have enabled the North to avoid South Korean defenses at the DMZ.

Initially, Pyongyang denied digging the tunnel but later claimed they had but the tunnel was a coal mine. Such a claim was illogical as no coal was found in the tunnel, primarily because rock formations there were granite—not sedimentary rock natural to coal formations. Never reluctant to tell a lie and certainly undeterred by geological science, the North then painted some tunnel walls black in an effort to suggest the existence of anthracite to support their claim.

This was not the only tunnel the South Koreans would discover, however.

In 1974, Seoul had learned through a North Korean defector who had been actively involved in the tunneling operations that other tunnels existed. South Korean troops bivouacking in the central sector of the DMZ in March 1975 became suspicious of popping sounds heard emanating from the ground beneath them. They reported what they heard up the chain of command. A squad was ordered to keep monitoring the activity, tracking its direction, noting the time of the sounds and determining any discernible patterns. The monitoring over the next few days left no doubt, the sounds clearly were heading further south, away from the DMZ.

Soon, other South Korean units patrolling the DMZ reported similar noises at numerous sites. The problem then became one of trying to locate the tunnels. It was a daunting task, but an engineering error by the tunnelers paid off for the South Koreans.

In excavating their tunnel, the North Koreans had dug too close to the surface. As a result, some dirt had fallen into a shaft near the bivouacked South Korean squad listening overhead. An alert South Korean soldier noticed heat waves rising up from the ground and the loose dirt around it. Using his bayonet to probe the hole, he saw more dirt crumble away. He fired his rifle into the shaft and immediately received return fire, followed by silence. The hole was widened so the tunnel could later be explored.

On March 19, 1975, the tunnel was entered and one twice the size of the first—seven feet by seven feet—was discovered. Its depth ranged from 160 to 500 feet and length extended about 3500 feet beyond the DMZ into South Korea. The tunnel was large enough to accommodate tanks and armored vehicles.

The discovery of the second tunnel, plus the sounds reported by other patrols of possible underground activity, launched a major initiative to locate other tunnels. Commercial drillers were brought in and, based on a technique involving the drilling of holes at various distances, triggering sound waves between them and then listening for the results to determine if open space existed between the holes, another tunnel was discovered.

This third tunnel was discovered in October 1978, proving to be almost identical to the second. A fourth was uncovered in March 1990.

The tunnels the North Koreans excavated proved to be more sophisticated as each new tunnel discovery was made. Newer tunnels were dug with a five-degree incline toward the south so water would collect on the North's side, where it would not interfere with drilling operations and could easily be pumped out.

The tunneling effort under the DMZ was the brain child of Kim Il Sung. He stated in motivating those responsible for building these roads down under that a single tunnel was worth ten nuclear bombs. It appears this message was lost on Kim Jong Il, who sought the nuclear bombs instead—although he too may be excavating tunnels as well.

It is not known how many more such tunnels remain to be found. Estimates are there may possibly be between 20-35 more. Each has but one purpose—to provide Pyongyang with an invasion route to penetrate the South's border and come up behind the DMZ, avoiding the most heavily defended border in the world. Ironically, some of these tunnels were probably dug underground as above ground South Korean leaders blindly sought to appease the North with its Sunshine Policy. But the tunnels are indicative of a clear mindset in the North that is committed to waging war rather than peace. With such a mindset engrained upon the North Korean military and its leadership, the chances for peace on the peninsula, as long as the Kim Dynasty rules, are slim.

The DMZ's "Flagpole War"

Also visible at the DMZ are enormous steel structures upon which fly the flags of both countries. As the "flagpole war" that erupted to give way to these structures is described, one can hear dueling banjos in the background.

In the 1980s, South Korea erected a 323 foot tall flagpole, the height of which necessitated a larger than normal size flag be flown. That flag, weighing almost 300 pounds, dwarfed the flag and flagpole on the

North's side. Not to be outdone, the North soon erected, what was at that time, the world's tallest flagpole. The North's flagpole was 525 feet tall from which a flag was flown weighing 595 pounds. Since the 1980s, other countries have sought their own world records, thus reducing both Korean flags to within the top five to ten tallest in the world. But the Flagpole War reflects a mindset easily offended. As such, Pyongyang's leadership sought to save face, expending millions of dollars for a flagpole when that money could have been better spent on improving the welfare of its people.

Is Kim Jong Un More Sensitive or Just a Leader Not Yet Hardened By the Reality of Power?

There is one trait, at least for the moment that distinguishes Kim Jong Un from his own father. Both Kim Jong Un's father and grandfather were not known as men of emotion or compassion. When his father died, Kim Jong Il showed no emotion, perhaps because the two men were believed to have been arguing at the time Kim Il Sung suffered his fatal heart attack. But, unlike his compassionless familial predecessors, Kim Jong Un has cried over the loss of his father. While his father's body lay in state, unlike Kim Jong Il did when Kim Il Sung died, Kim Jong Un has made numerous trips to pay his respects.

It is much too early to know if the incident reveals a more sensitive member of the Kim dynasty has evolved.

But, even if he has, he still will be faced with the realities of running the gauntlet of North Korea's brutal power infrastructure—an exercise that may well extinguish any such sensitivity.

Will Kim Jong Un Be Haunted by the Ghost of Kim Jong Il Past As Kim Jong Il Was Haunted by the Ghost of Kim Il Sung Past?

Of interest as well will be whether Kim Jong Un feels any need to compete against the ghost of his father as Kim Jong Il felt the need to compete against the ghost of his.

A museum was built during Kim Il Song's lifetime to honor him by putting on display for the North Korean public the thousands of gifts he had received. In a great hall of the building stands a very life-like statue of the Great Leader. There is, as well, a sign that was periodically changed during his lifetime, to show the total tally of gifts on display.

A newer museum directly across the street from his father's now houses all gifts on display that were given to Kim Jong Il. Similar to the father's museum, the son's life-like statue stands, with an electronic sign, immediately registering each gift as it was received. Visiting the two buildings left no doubt in the mind of outside observers the son was driven by a need to compete with a father whom he sought to excel.

Despite some animosity between the two Kims, Kim Jong Il was smart enough to recognize he had to do all he could to promote his father's legacy in order to preserve and succeed to his power base as his father's successor.

Kim Jong Il made it a state policy to honor his father as the country's "Eternal President." Today, Kim Il Sung is revered among North Koreans as the single most respected leader. That esteem will become even more evident in April 2012 as the country celebrates in great grandeur and at tremendous expense, despite a starving population, Kim Il Song's 100th birthday. The main beneficiaries of the event will be the elite for whom expensive luxury items are already being imported, which will be used to help buy their political support. A cash-strapped North Korea can be counted on to increase its drug marketing, weapons proliferation and foreign currency (primarily US) counterfeiting activities to be able to pay its bills.

Kim Jong Il Would Have Made His Father Proud

In at least one area of government-sanctioned activity, Kim Jong Il was successful where his father was not. Understanding Kim Il Sung's keen interest in the illegal activity, his son's success at it undoubtedly would have "done his father proud"—but such is the perverse world of dictators untethered by any moral code.

To raise badly needed cash for his regime, Kim Il Sung was enticed by an Asian drug lord to grow poppies, cultivating them to produce heroin. At the time of Kim Il Sung's death, a massive supply of heroin sat unsold, housed in a building just outside Pyongyang proper as the original drug lord involved had disappeared. One of the first actions ordered by Kim Jong Il after coming to power was for the military to establish a relationship with a cartel to market the heroin. This was done at a handsome profit to Pyongyang. Kim Jong Il therefore decided to commit valuable, but limited, arable land in the country to grow poppies, denying a starving population the acreage to grow crops and feed themselves. As profits from an ambitious international drug trade came in, much of it went into Kim Jong Il's personal foreign bank account or to fund the country's nuclear program.

On the day of Kim Jong Il's funeral, the North Korean Worker's Party newspaper credited among the Dear Leader's greatest achievements the nuclear weapons and long range missile technology programs he authorized. Justifying the program, the newspaper said, "Thanks to these legacies, we do not worry about the destiny of ourselves and posterity at this time of national mourning." Unmentioned was the fact Kim Jong Il's policies had left a nation so weakened by malnutrition, its people undoubtedly, should the need arise, would have difficulty mounting a prolonged defense in time of crisis.

Influence of the Chinese Dragon

While the extent of its influence over Pyongyang is questionable, the land of the dragon is clearly the one nation in a position to wield the most influence upon the new regime. It is clear that China's desire for a transition of power in North Korea's leadership is one that would ensure stability on the peninsula.

China has played the role of facilitator among a group of countries that have long been engaged in negotiations with North Korea—negotiations known as the Six Party Talks. These on-again-off-again negotiations involving the two Koreas, Japan, Russia, China and the US tend to be more off than on-again as Pyongyang has repeatedly disrupts them, usually be committing an unprovoked act of aggression.

The talks were on-again before Kim Jong Il's death. While a deal was close to being hammered out in which Pyongyang would discontinue its uranium production program in exchange for food, there is really never a comfort level within the international community that North Korea will truly honor the terms it accepts. Meanwhile, China constantly excuses Pyongyang's aggressiveness, encouraging all to return to the talks.

Most often, the victim of North Korea's aggression is its neighbor to the South. Never a victim itself, China continuously plays the role of the North's defender and big brother. While Beijing encourages Pyongyang to tone things down, even with China North Korea can prove to be a rogue brother. Eventually, all parties re-engage, at least until the cycle repeats itself. If a sign of insanity is for one to keep doing the same thing in expectation of a different outcome, then five of the Six Party talk participants clearly suffer from insanity. Ironically, the nation best known for insanity—North Korea—fails to meet this definition as it never expects a different outcome. The five other participants never disappoint, repeatedly rewarding Pyongyang each time for its belligerence with shipments of food and oil. Meanwhile, the international community's reward is Pyongyang's broken promises to stop its nuclear arms program.

China will be content to continue in this role as long as it succeeds in keeping North Korea intact. It could care less about Pyongyang becoming a more responsible member of the community of nations. It could care less about Pyongyang implementing economic reform to improve life for its own citizens. It could care less about North Korea selling nuclear technology to other states with interests opposed to those of the US. As evidenced by Beijing's support in the past for Iraq's Saddam Hussein, Libya's Muammar Gaddafi, Iran's Mahmoud Ahmadinejad and Syria's Bashar Assad, it has yet to find a dictator it does not like. Such support is especially important for China as North Korea's collapse—and a subsequent unification of the Koreas—would place US forces, now stationed in South Korea, directly on China's border. With President Barack Obama's recent announcement the US would start directing its foreign policy efforts at a region of the world it has long neglected—Asia—Beijing sees the fall of the Kim dynasty and subsequent removal of the North as a buffer to US troops as a serious affront to its prestige.

In the years since Kim Jong Il's 2008 stroke, Beijing worked on developing a solid relationship with Kim Jong Un's uncle, Jang Sung Taek. It will seek to further solidify that relationship by promoting Kim Jong Un's transition of power and by encouraging other countries to do the same.

Accordingly, under the Chinese dragon's protective umbrella, Kim Jong Un will make a smooth transition to power. It is an umbrella that means yet another generation of North Koreans is doomed to suffer in darkness just to ensure stability on the peninsula for China's benefit.

An Unfinished Hotel Reveals a "Need to Lie" Mentality

As the power struggle plays out in North Korea and observers try to assess what is going on, we must recognize an aspect of the North Korean diplomatic mindset best explained, perhaps, by the following story.

Upon the author's first trip to Pyongyang in 1994, the most visible building on the city's skyline was the 105-story Ryugyong Hotel. The building was clearly unfinished then, with inactive construction equipment visible at ground level. When the author inquired about the status of its construction, he was informed construction was still in progress. But, during the author's last trip to Pyongyang in 2004, it was clear no additional progress had been made in ten years. After inquiring again about the hotel's status, he was again told it was still under construction. That was more than other North Koreans would say as most would not even acknowledge its existence.

Construction had begun in 1987 with the building to be a showcase hotel for North Korea. Construction stopped in 1992 due to major engineering problems for which the North Koreans refused to seek outside assistance. The hotel was abandoned, with decades of cold weather taking its toll on the building. In an effort to save face, Pyongyang officials continue to claim it is under construction or totally avoid the subject. Not even David Copperfield could make this monstrosity disappear, leaving it as a major source of embarrassment for North Koreans unwilling to admit its engineering flaws.

For years, visitors wondered what would collapse first—the hotel or the Kim dynasty!

Now, after lying dormant for more than two decades, the hotel has sprung to life—albeit partially. It appears Pyongyang finally succeeded in obtaining a foreign investment partner to help complete the building. Slated to open in mid-2012, only the lower portion of the building will be completed—and not as a hotel but for office use. North Korea was hopeful they could open the building up in time to commemorate the 100th birthday of Kim Il Sung, but that will not happen at the current construction rate. The fact Pyongyang has rejected less costly plans—by other potential investors who examined the property—to tear down the "cement mountain," as the Ryugyong has been called, to start all over demonstrates the inability of the North Korean government ever to acknowledge it has made a mistake.

But the Ryugyong Hotel provides us with an insight into the North Korean diplomatic mindset which focuses on denying even that which is most obvious. There is a "need to lie" to prevent any negativity from reflecting back on the leadership, even if it is inconsequential or a product of innocent mistake. It is important we understand this as a new leader, but one with the same mindset, transitions into power.

Returning to the question as to whether the Ryugyong or the Kim dynasty will collapse first, both have received new life. The people of North Korea can withstand decades more of the former, but can they of the latter?

The Nuclear Issue—"Who Will Dance if We Have War?"

Nowhere has the "need to deceive" been heeded more than what is known about Pyongyang's nuclear weapons program. The author received a taste of this deception during his first trip to North Korea.

In 1994, the author was part of an international delegation invited to Pyongyang. The question on every one's mind was whether North Korea possessed nuclear weapons. At a luncheon hosted by Kim Il Sung, the question was directly put to him.

Despite exhibiting a very warm side for most of the two hour lunch, he became visibly annoyed by the inquiry. He emphatically stated, "We will never have nuclear weapons. Who would we use them against? Why have nuclear weapons when we are surrounded by big powers that have them?"

Referencing the horrors of nuclear war, he asked, "You have seen our city. We have no desire to have it destroyed. You saw my birthday celebration last night with thousands of dancers. Who will dance if we have war?"

It was interesting Kim Il Sung asked more questions of those in the delegation on the matter than were asked of him. It would appear the response he wanted those present to hear was one he never shared with his son based on the nuclear weapons program advanced under Kim Jong Il's later leadership. And, under a third generation of the Kim Dynasty, there is little to suggest Kim Jong Un is eager to halt the program.

There is one point Kim Il Sung made in response to possessing nuclear weapons that may have had an element of truth in it. He said, "You have seen our city. We have no desire to see it destroyed." As Kim Dynasty members have enjoyed a luxurious lifestyle, they undoubtedly do not want to risk a nuclear conflict that would deny that lifestyle to them. Therefore, it is highly unlikely the Dynasty will run the risk of doing so by launching a nuclear strike. The real concern, however, is that they continue to sell and transfer their technology to countries much more willing to do so.

We should not be surprised, however, to see Kim Jong Un quickly master North Korea's time-honored foreign policy of promising everything and delivering on nothing. In this vein, we may well see him promise to halt his nuclear arms program—only throttling back long enough to gain economic concessions from South Korea and the US before moving forward again. The sale of the technology remains too much of a cash cow for Pyongyang to totally surrender the program.

Is Truth a Casualty Concerning the Real Circumstances of Kim Jong Il's Death?

Truth always bends to propaganda opportunities in the North, even when it would seem not to matter. Even now, the details released by Pyongyang about Kim Jong Il's death have raised questions. Reports indicated he died on his train while traveling on a "field guidance" tour. However, satellite photos reveal the train never even left the station, suggesting the Dear Leader was at his Pyongyang residence at the time of death. Perhaps the picture of him dying while at play there did not quite fit into the cultist image of him dying while at work on the country's problems. The leader's extensive library of thousands of Western films and videos of all shows ever performed by some entertainers, such as Japanese magician Princess Tenko who attended his funeral at Pyongyang's request, would indicate he was spending more time at play than at work.

It is also important to bear in mind that there is not a single agreement Pyongyang has yet made that it has not broken—no matter how major or minor the commitment. The reciprocal summit meetings are just one in a long line. And, while those meetings gave the international community renewed hope of improved relations, it was only learned Pyongyang's sole motivation to meet was a one billion dollar cash payment South Korean President Dae Jung Kim secretly paid the North.

Trusting North Korea Requires a "Smith Barney" Approach

The international community, including China, was caught by surprise by the death of Kim Jong Il—only learning about it two days after it occurred via Pyongyang's official announcement. Obviously, there is a clear lack of human intelligence available in assessing and predicting what will happen next within the Hermit

Kingdom. Little wonder why North Korea is an intelligence analyst's worst nightmare.

While we will constantly be left to assess a range of numerous indicators to interpret what may be going on, we also need to recognize no public declaration by Pyongyang can be accepted at face value. This is an important consideration should the Six Party talks continue and an agreement concerning North Korea's nuclear program be reached.

The signature phrase used by Ronald Reagan during the Cold War concerning strategic agreements with the Soviet Union was "trust but verify." With North Korea, however, we must totally ignore the trust factor for it simply is not a part of its culture. Just like the investment firm of Smith Barney advertises it gains the respect of clients by proving its success the old-fashioned way—i.e., "earning" it by making money for them—trust for North Korea needs to be established the same way—i.e., Pyongyang has to earn it. Therefore, any future agreement with the North Koreas demands complete verification—with Pyongyang attaching no strings. It is doubtful a young Kim Jong Un will demonstrate weakness by agreeing to any such accord.

South Korean President Lee has suggested, "If North Korea shows an attitude of sincerity, a new era on the Korean peninsula can be opened. Should a Kim Jong Un regime make such a pitch to South Korea and the US, there is a simple test that can be administered to measure Pyongyang's sincerity. It was a test administered recently by Secretary of State Hillary Clinton to determine whether the leadership of another country known for its brutal authoritarian rule for nearly a quarter of a century—Burma—was serious about political reforms.

Before Clinton would agree to meet with Burmese officials and discuss US cooperation, she wanted the government to release hundreds of political prisoners. Suffering from a dire economic situation, Burma realized after years of repressing its people, the onus was on it to demonstrate to the outside world it was serious about reform. True to its word, it did so, garnering US trust and a promise to establish a US ambassador there.

A similar demand of Pyongyang would be most revealing about North Korea's intentions. But, based on the Kim Dynasty's need to live the *juche* lie and promote the cult persona of its leadership, it is extremely doubtful such a release would ever occur. The concern by Pyongyang in doing so is that it runs the danger of corrupting its stranglehold over its people by planting the seeds of hope in a very malleable North Korean population ignorant of the fact a better life lies just beyond their borders.

While Initial Transition Signs Support Stability, as for North Korea's Future, the Lights Will Remain Out

Following the announcement of Kim Jong Il's death, Pyongyang quickly shut down the country's borders. The fact those borders were then, just as quickly, re-opened bodes well for stability for Kim Jong Un's transition to power. This decision, as well as the one to test-fire a missile two days after Kim Jong Il's death indicates decisions of consequence are being made without much hesitation. Someone is wielding the power of a head-of-state or working with Kim Jong Un to do so.

A NASA satellite photograph taken at night many years ago of the entire Korean peninsula is very telling. It shows the half of the peninsula occupied by democratic South Korea lit up like a Christmas tree as the half occupied by communist North Korea is shrouded in darkness. The photograph is an ominous reflection of the human spirit that exists on either side of the DMZ. It speaks volumes as to the impact a single family's leadership has had in the north where it has refused to lead its people out of darkness. It is doubtful a future NASA photograph, taken a few years from now, will reflect any change. Illuminating the north by turning the lights on for their people just conflicts too much with the Kim cult persona to be a viable alternative for Pyongyang's leadership.

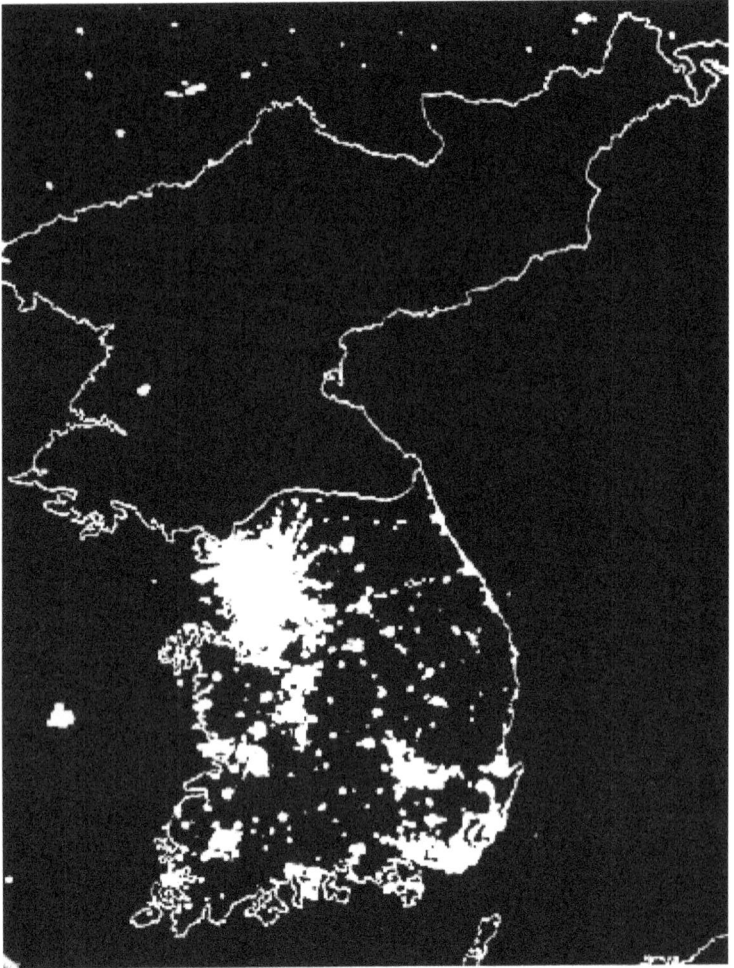

It is said Kim Jong Il selected his youngest son as successor because he most resembled him in image and personality. If so, and the son proves to be like the father, things do not bode well not only for the North Korean people who will continue to live in darkness but for freedom-loving South Koreans hoping to break their northern brothers free from the yoke of the Kim dynasty.

About the Author:

Lieutenant Colonel James Zumwalt is a retired Marine infantry officer who served in the Vietnam war, the 1989 intervention into Panama and Desert Storm. An internationally acclaimed best-selling author, speaker and business executive, he also currently heads a security consulting firm named after his father—Admiral Zumwalt & Consultants, Inc.

He writes extensively on foreign policy and defense issues, having written hundreds of articles for various newspapers and magazines, including USA Today, The Washington Post, The New York Times, The Washington Times, The LA Times, The Chicago Tribune, The San Diego Union, Parade magazine and others. His articles have covered issues of major importance, oftentimes providing readers with unique perspectives that have never appeared elsewhere. This has resulted, on several occasions, in his work being cited by members of Congress and entered into the US Congressional Record.

His thoughtful perspectives earned him an invitation to join the prestigious Committee on the Present Danger (CPD), of which the honorary co-chairmen are Senator Joe Lieberman, Senator Jon Kyl, former Secretary of State George P. Schultz and former CIA Director R. James Woolsey. The CPD is a non-partisan organization with one goal—to stiffen American resolve to confront the challenge presented by terrorism and the ideologies that drive it.

Colonel Zumwalt is featured as one of 56 US military professionals in LEADING THE WAY, a book by best-selling author Al Santoli, which documents the most critical moments of the interviewees' combat experiences from Vietnam to Somalia.

He has also been cited in numerous other books and publications for unique insights based on his research on the Vietnam war, North Korea (a country he has visited ten times and about which he is able to share some very telling observations) and Desert Storm.

Colonel Zumwalt received a presidential appointment to be the Senior Advisor to the Assistant Secretary of State for Human Rights and Humanitarian Affairs, in which capacity he served from 1991-1992.

Because of his expertise, he also was asked to participate in a very unique educational project conducted at a high school in Raleigh, North Carolina, where he voluntarily contributes time and resources to educating students on issues of international importance.

He is the author of "Bare Feet, Iron Will ~ Stories from the Other Side of Vietnam's Battlefields". He is also a contributor to Rear Admiral Greg Slavonic's book, "Leadership In Action | Principles Forged in the Crucible of Military Service Can Lead Corporate America Back to the Top".

www.ingramcontent.com/pod-product-compliance
Lightning Source LLC
Chambersburg PA
CBHW021337290326
41933CB00038B/905